Marriage in action

Marital activities and marriage maintenance

Mia Lily

Table of Contents

Chapter 1

Today's problem in marriage

You were deeply in love, more than eager to spend the rest of your life with your spouse, and ready to go to any lengths to ensure their happiness every day.
Yes, you listened to all the advice that happily married people gave you, and you remember hearing that a successful marriage required a lot of effort and had its share of happy and unhappy moments. You had anticipated that you two would be the perfect wedded pair.

Imagine yourself a few years in the future, maybe alone in a hotel room. You don't speak to your spouse much, or if you do, it takes a lot to keep from fighting. Perhaps you think everything they say is a jab or an insult. You fight so often that you can't recall

the last time you spent a day without having a contentious discussion.
Your sexual life is either nonexistent or suffering. In the middle of the night, while you lie in bed, you ponder how you got here and how you're ever going to get out.

Relationship issues may be emotionally taxing and very isolating.

Identifying typical marriage issues
It's crucial to keep in mind that most marriages have difficulties; you are not alone in this.

Marital issues and how to work through them with your partner to move on toward a happy life together.

1. Money
It should come as no surprise that money is the primary cause of the majority of marital issues. Our lives depend on money, and when there isn't enough of it to cover our

needs, everyone is put under a tremendous amount of stress. In addition, if there is poor financial communication or if one partner is dishonest about where they are spending money, there may be major trust difficulties that affect other aspects of the marriage.

2. Closeness
Many married couples believe that as time passes, their sexual lives grow less stimulating. Both partners may experience emotions of inadequacy and uncertainty when our interactions get more infrequent and further between.

3. Unwanted Friends
Even friends may cause discord. Even though it isn't often discussed with marital problems. It may cause a lot of conflict between spouses if the friends of one spouse don't get along with those of the other. This becomes a concern in particular if such

friendships begin to take priority over marriage or family.

4. Domestic Work Division

Do you believe you're in charge of the bulk of the household's logistics, cooking, cleaning, and organizing? Is there much disagreement between you and your spouse as a result of it? It's not just you. You're coping with one of the most prevalent marriage issues right now.

5. Parental Disparities

If you have kids, you already know how important it is for you and your spouse to take care of them and their needs. Even if your children are at the center of everything you do, your spouse and you may not always share the same parenting philosophies. In terms of discipline, establishing and keeping routines, and many other facets of parenting, you could come across significant variances. Conflicts continue and escalate as a result of this.

6. Dependence
If a spouse's significant addiction issue isn't handled appropriately and with enough help, it may be a major cause of stress and tension. Marriage troubles are brought on by more than just addiction; they may also be exceedingly difficult to resolve due to dishonesty, financial difficulties, and other factors.

7.Even though we consent to become one when we get married, married couples are still two different persons. Everybody in a partnership provides their viewpoint, experiences, emotions, and sentiments. Many of the typical marriage issues mentioned above have their roots in poor communication. People must practice successful communication over time, and often, they need expert advice to learn how to listen to one another.

making marital issues less prevalent

You are not alone if your marriage is having problems. Not needing assistance in resolving typical marital issues is not a sign of shame. Instead, demonstrating your readiness to do so demonstrates your dedication to a happy and successful marriage. Everyone sometimes needs a little assistance, and those who ask for it often find themselves in a much better situation and a happier marriage.

Chapter 2

Detox your marriage

We enter a relationship to feel secure in the sentiments that the other person feels for us. Together with that particular individual who is extremely important to us, we want to enjoy life and live it to the utmost.

However, some individuals are not interested in you, and as time goes on, their motives begin to shift. We can see a clear shift in their views, behaviors, and treatment of their spouse, whom they formerly had a strong affection for!

Such a stage causes the sensations to start deteriorating and the magic that once connected them to begin to fade.

This is known as "toxicity." To put it another way, your relationship has become toxic, which is very harmful and hazardous to both your mind and body.

We should thus make an effort to avoid engaging in behavior that depletes our energy.

Here are five strategies for revitalizing a relationship and rekindling the flame that previously burned there.

1. You must voice your worries.
Perhaps the other person is going through some personal struggles, which is why his opinions are shifting. How may a relationship be made clean? Let him or her know what is upsetting you to start.

Where do you believe the situation has changed? They must be made aware of this. It's conceivable that they are not conscious of the abrupt changes in their conduct that you have seen.

2. Commit to yourself

It's crucial to take good care of oneself. Most individuals tend to forget that they need to love themselves, particularly when they are in a relationship.

Yes! It's crucial to take good care of oneself. Realize your value. Never settle for anything less. You are flawless, therefore there is no need to make concessions; furthermore, you can find a better spouse.

Simply be kind to yourself and recognize all the unique qualities that make you unique.

3. Motivate change
You should lead by example by changing other people. Take the following actions to motivate your partner to alter their behavior and end the relationship.

To avoid a bad response, regularly check in with yourself before acting: Stopping and reflecting before responding takes work and experience. You'll be astounded at how quickly your brain and body support your decision to alter your reactions, however, if you do this regularly.

Ensure that you are being your best self:

Regardless of whether you believe you have never come into contact with a toxic version of yourself, focus only on becoming the greatest version of yourself. When you are dealing with the toxic behavior of your life partner, this approach will help you to lessen your poisonous behavior and choose a more honorable course of action.

4. Interact with your pals.

the other pals you have.

Keep in mind that one buddy with whom you have not spoken since entering this relationship. Call that buddy and discuss your life with them. Meet the rest of your pals.

Be sociable and make friends; they will assist you and provide you advice on how to purge your connection.

5.To make marriage last forever Look in the mirror

You may be the source of the issue and are unable to recognize it. Breathe in deeply. If you like writing, you may record everything in a diary.

Ask someone for help since they can identify your limitations and be more honest with you about your shortcomings than you can.

Before pointing out flaws in your relationship, strive to improve any areas that need improvement. Maybe the fluctuations in your conduct caused your lover to alter his perspective toward you!

That is only an idea. Do give it some thought.

6. Maintain a healthy schedule

While developing wholesome routines and habits is necessary and beneficial in many areas of life, it's also good to sometimes try something new.

Enjoy yourself; begin writing, drawing, or whatever other creative endeavor strikes your fancy.

Pick a pastime that inspires your creative side, and you'll feel energized and content. Yoga walks, and other forms of exercise should be done sometimes each day.

You will be able to cleanse your spirit as well as the suffering you endured throughout that poisonous relationship by doing this.

Watch the TED presentation below to learn more about the surprising power of rituals, routines, and habits.

7. Seek aid

Many folks are completely clueless about what to do. Our society lacks knowledge of relationship detox.

Fixing a toxic marriage or ending unhealthy relationships is no easy task. It might be difficult to find an answer to the question of how to detoxify a relationship.

The greatest course of action, whether it be to leave a toxic relationship or learn how to detox your relationship, is to obtain qualified help—someone who can provide you with the knowledge of the most effective way to detox relationships.

Marriage therapy or relationship guidance from an outside, unbiased professional who can help you recognize the warning signs of a toxic relationship, mend strained relationships by establishing certain ground rules, and motivate you to move on from a toxic relationship.

Getting knowledge on the best way to detox relationships or hiring a professional to assist you in the process would be a huge step towards the couple's recovery from the destructive marriage or changing your partner's destructive behavior.

The last observation

There are just two options available to you: either work on the relationship and resolve it or let go; the former is difficult. However, it depends on your circumstances and if you and your partner are sincere about one another and want to keep the relationship going or not.

It won't function if you push it to. Just move on and live your life as the greatest version of yourself if it feels like things are not going your way.

Chapter 3

How to cope with your loved one in marriage

Relationships: Partners and spouses
A marriage must be nurtured, grown, and protected. It might sometimes feel tough to keep up that collaboration with job schedules, kids, and other responsibilities. Some couples discover that divorcing and moving apart is better when issues occur. 1

For some people, improving the relationship is a preferable option. There are proactive steps you may take if you want to remain married and prevent divorce. The following ten suggestions can help you strengthen your relationship, from increasing communication to adding more romance to your routine.

1.Divorce and Annulment: Their Differences
Keep Your Relationship a Priority
Even if you never say it out loud, toying with the notion that you could be happier elsewhere can cause serious tension in your relationships. Just the concept of it might seriously undermine your desire to work on strengthening your marriage.

2.

Make up your mind in advance that divorce is not an option to reduce the danger to your partnership. Committing will enable you to concentrate on strengthening your relationship rather than imagining a life apart.

Respect and Honor Your Partner
Inevitably, people evolve throughout time. Any partnership must comprehend, appreciate, and adjust to such changes. To start, list your spouse's greatest traits to serve as a constant reminder of the amazing person you married. You'll be able to recall

your first feelings for them thanks to this activity.
It also helps to express how much you value your partner's idiosyncrasies and oddities.

3.Express your appreciation for all your spouse does every day by giving them praises or saying "thank you."

These little expressions are like bank deposits. You shouldn't take money out of your marriage without ever putting anything in. So, make sure your actions respect your spouse for who they are.

Keep in touch often
It's simple to get sidetracked in the era of smartphones, Netflix, and work-from-home arrangements. You can discover that you often have days without a sincere discussion with your partner.

Fostering closeness in a partnership requires honest communication about one's life, hobbies, aspirations, disappointments, and emotions.

4.

It's also important that you pay attention to what your spouse has to say. Setting aside 30 minutes each day to communicate without interruptions or distractions might be beneficial.

Share Your Financial Goals

Financial disputes are a common source of tension in marriages.

5. Different expectations around money are often brought into relationships by couples. It might be challenging for each spouse to understand the financial position from the other's point of view.

A good marriage depends on you and your spouse coming to an understanding of how your finances will be managed. Make a plan to live within your means and come to an agreement on a budget and debt repayment strategy.

Making the distinction between necessities and desires is also crucial. Both are OK, but if a couple tries to satisfy every want without taking their budget into account, issues may arise.

Include some wiggle room in your spending plan to include entertainment, presents, trips, and other things that will improve your marriage.

Give one another room

The ideal amount of time to spend with your spouse is one of the most challenging things to balance in a marriage. When there is too little or too much, it might seem inattentive or oppressive.

Offer to keep the kids or do errands when your spouse requests some alone time or a night out with friends to make sure they can. On the other side, you should also schedule time for your relationship with your spouse. If childcare difficulties or a lack of money prevent that, organize a pleasant, affordable date night at home.

The important thing is that you both make an effort to spend quality time together while still giving each other room to have a separate social life.

6.

Promote wellness

Being excessively casual might become a habit, particularly if you've been seeing your partner for a while. Remembering the early stages of dating, such as having a home manicure before a date, getting a new haircut and shaving, or picking out nice clothing, might help to reignite passion.

There are several methods to feel energizing and appealing. Maintaining your physical fitness increases your feeling of well-being and self-confidence.

7.

Whether you're attempting a new exercise class, preparing for a 5K, or spending time preparing nutritious meals with your spouse, it may also be a chance to spend quality time together.

Take Your Date Out

Continue wooing your spouse as a strategy to maintain the spark in your marriage.

8 Try to schedule a date night at least once every week, even if it's only to grab an ice cream or try a new meal.

If cost is a barrier, talk to another couple that wants to go on a date night about exchanging childcare. Simply strap the infant into a stroller and stroll around the mall or to the park.

Keep acting in the same manner that you did while you were dating. Many couples claim that doing little, kind gestures makes them feel like newlyweds.

Try making your spouse coffee in the morning, buying their favorite food at the grocery store, or placing tiny love notes where they will find them.

Let go quickly
When one spouse harbors resentment, marriages often start to disintegrate. According to research, harboring resentment against your spouse nearly always festers and, if left unattended, may result in divorce. 9

As soon as you can, try to forgive your lover. Keep in mind that extending forgiveness is a gift you offer to yourself as well. Maintaining resentment consumes mental and emotional energy and nearly always has a negative influence on your health and stress levels. 10

If you choose to be forgiving, you will experience favorable results, such as less stress or better sleep.

Ask your partner's forgiveness and provide an honest apology if you have hurt them. Pay attention to what they have to say and make an effort to comprehend their point of contention. Inform them that you are working on future procedures to be different.

Never attempt to manipulate your partner. Both spouses respect one another and don't insist on getting their way in a happy marriage. Although individual couples may interpret this differently, the following fundamental ideas should be kept in mind:

Avoid attempting to manage or watch one another.
Allow your spouse to be themselves.
Learn to work together on important choices (such as spending money and raising children).
Allow your spouse to enter and exit the house without your consent.

Controlling partners run the danger of developing emotional abuse. The possibility of financial abuse, which commonly results in divorce, may be present.

Find Support

Consider counseling or couples therapy if your marriage is still experiencing issues or if you think divorce may be on the horizon.

11

If you're unsure of where to search, start by asking around at work. Check to see whether you (or your significant other) have access to an employee assistance program (EAP), which often may point you in the direction of first support or make a recommendation.

If you and your partner are religious, you may want to consult with a reputable clergyman.

Does Marriage Therapy Work?

Message From Verywell

In a marriage, navigating problems may be difficult.
Both parties must be willing to put in the time and effort necessary to maintain the relationship and avoid divorce. Although saving the relationship is the main objective, you will eventually need to determine whether remaining together is best for both of you.

Consider meeting with a marital therapist or a religious leader if you and your spouse need more assistance. These people can assist you in gaining fresh insight and, if necessary, can direct you toward other services.

Chapter 4

To make marriage last forever

Everyone aspires to have the happiest marriage possible. You want someone who will always love you, someone with whom you can have fun, and most importantly, someone with whom you can live a happy, full life.

You commit to love your spouse through good and terrible circumstances on your wedding day. However, there are occasions when the bad far surpasses the good, and as a result, marriages fail. However, there are several things you can do to ensure the longevity of your blissful union:

1. Set aside time for one another
The most priceless gift you can offer your love is your time. Making time will mean so

much to the two of you since you both are aware of each other's hectic schedules.

2. Give each other priority

Put your relationship first, above anything else, including your children. If you and your partner are continually at odds, your family cannot be healthy. Therefore, put your relationship first.

3. Compliment each other.

Sincere compliments between a husband and wife may go a long way. Tell your sweetie what you find admirable in them.

4. Make physical contact a regular occurrence.

Every relationship has to have some level of physical contact. To accomplish this, you don't need to be intimate all the time; just a gentle touch on the shoulder or a tender handshake would enough.

5. Talk to others

Never stop exchanging ideas. Maintain consistency. Always make sure your partner is aware of your feelings. The greatest thing you can do for your marriage is probably to maintain open lines of communication.

6. Be fearless when you disagree.
It's quite common for couples to dispute. Set limits for your disputes to make sure you're not harming each other, but don't entirely dismiss issues.

Remove your expectations.
Unmet expectations are the leading cause of divorce. Other than that, no marriage is the same, so it's better to set aside your expectations at this time. You should anticipate your fundamental requirements to be satisfied.

8. Give yourself some time.
To be the best spouse you can be, you need to take the time to feed and care for yourself.

9. Discover how to apologize and accept them
Your marriage won't be joyful if you don't learn to say sorry and forgive. You'll let each other down, but if you forgive and apologize right away, it will be much better.

10. Keep personal issues secret.
Do not vent your concerns about your marriage to your 20 closest friends. Keep it between the two of you and, if necessary, a therapist.

11. Avoid contrasting your marriage.
Do not contrast your marriage with those of the well-known Instagram influencers you follow since every marriage is unique. Your marriage is successful for you, and that ought to be sufficient.

12. Acknowledge that your partner cannot read your thoughts.

Your lover doesn't know what you're thinking, and the only way they will be aware of it is if you express it.

13. Don't criticize your spouse

It's improper to criticize your significant other in any way. Don't post Facebook posts that are passively antagonistic, and don't complain to your pals about how unpleasant your spouse has been recent. To solve such issues, have a conversation with one another.

14. Always make an effort to win your spouse over

You shouldn't stop trying to impress your partner just because you're married. Continue dressing up, reminding them how much you value them, and expressing your affection for them.

15. Ensure that you are close buddies.

You acquired the best buddy for life when you married your spouse. You should never take advantage of this fantastic offer for granted.

Your marriage will become stronger and you two will be together forever if you put in real effort every day.

Chapter 5

How to keep marriage perfectly

Three Tips for a Successful Marriage
Whether or whether you are aware of these secrets will determine whether your marriage succeeds.

Years have been spent by me working on my spiritual development, coaching, and counseling. I have also invested years in my marriage via training, spiritual development, and therapy.

Considering these factors, I have to admit that marriage requires a lot of effort. You and your spouse may have a deep experience when you put your money and time into the appropriate channels and endeavors.

Although there is a lot of material on this topic, I have discovered several straightforward procedures that, when followed, will help your relationship go on the proper path. There are a few important, basic things to keep in mind.

guy kisses a lady in a white shirt while wearing a black leather jacket.

A marriage relationship, for instance, is a relationship.
I like to compare relationships to plants when I think about them. I suppose I tend to consider a lot of things as plants... Reverting to plants For plants to survive, they need the following seven factors. They need space, the right temperature, light, water, air, nutrients, and enough time to flourish.

Similar to plants, marriages need a certain combination of elements to develop and survive. Try reading The Seven Principles for Making Marriage Work by Dr. John

Gottman for a comprehensive look at this subject. You should buy and read this book, in my opinion.

Just keep in mind that if you want your relationship to thrive, you must take care of it just as you would any other living creature. The married bond is what I prefer to think of as a first child. It is a living entity that requires a lot of tenderness, love, and giving.

The Ingredients in Secret (Necessities).
I feel like I can give some keys to a successful marriage after 20 years of marriage to my wonderful wife, lessons learned, healed scars, four degrees, many hours spent counseling others, and continuing relational involvement in my marriage.

The three main requirements are:

Physical intimacy in sex

Information Sharing and Intellectual Intimacy
Emotional intimacy and trust

1. Great sex needs more than just physical prowess.
Intimacy is essential to having great sex. I refer to relational, spiritual, emotional, and physical intimacy when I use the term "intimacy."
Many unmarried couples believe that the honeymoon is the only time to have excellent sex.

The honeymoon serves as the couple's first experience with marital sex. Compared to other forms of sex you may have had, married sex is unique. Because wonderful sex requires closeness, it is the cause of the problem.

Genuine trust and a strong emotional connection are necessary for great sex. After

several years of dedication to one another, this occurs.
I imagined having a fantastic sexual experience with my wife on our honeymoon. What I didn't anticipate were the sentiments, the protracted conversations, the senses of uneasiness, and the disagreements. We had our first significant marriage argument when we were on our honeymoon.

This is something I've seen that is fairly typical with newlyweds. To have excellent sex, work on building an emotional connection with your partner. This is accomplished via trust and communication.

2. Effective communication goes beyond words.
According to research, nonverbal communication accounts for 70 to 90% of all communication. Seriously, give it some time to sit before you think about it. Nonverbal indicators include body language,

tone, and micro- and macro-communications. Talking alone is not communication. Women use more words than males, according to studies, so how can we communicate most effectively? rather than "how many words do we use?" When a couple is working on communication problems, they use words, but not in a manner that allows them to express their true feelings.

This has to do with their incapacity to relate to their own emotions since they don't understand themselves well enough to be able to communicate what's going on. Another possibility is that they don't trust their partner with their emotions. The problem of inadequate communication may go beyond these two causes. People may struggle with PTSD or trauma from their early years.

Whatever the situation, improving communication is necessary for the couple to achieve a healthy and vibrant relationship. I want to reassure you that you can get through the problems I've described. It will call for dedication and perseverance.

3. Significant trust is gained.
Your capacity to believe something defines your level of trust. Your capacity to believe in your spouse constitutes trust in a relationship.

Having the capacity to gain and maintain trust is one of the keys to a happy marriage. The foundation of a happy marriage is trust. Your marriage will suffer without it.

Trust is essential for healthy partnerships. Without trust, you cannot have a real connection.
If you can't learn to trust one another, your relationship is doomed. This remark serves as a wake-up call rather than a death

sentence. Address any suspicion or mistrust you may be feeling in your relationship.

Trust is brittle and difficult to rebuild. Respecting your spouse and doing your bit to be dependable and trustworthy are essential components of maintaining trust.

Chapter 6

A happy and healthy marriage

Each couple has many goals and ambitions for their future life together, along with their family and friends. But getting married happily is by no means an easy journey. And many couples decide not to finish the voyage, as today's divorce rates all too clearly show.

It would be simple to attribute our high incidence of divorce to neglecting to spend enough time together, allowing anger and hatred to fester, and failing to maintain open channels of communication.

You may learn how to enhance these and several other elements of your relationship through a variety of books, articles, and seminars. Although spending quality time together, forgiving one another, and having open lines of communication are essential to a good marriage, if these things aren't occurring, it's often an indication of a far bigger issue. Furthermore, no amount of external behavior adjustment will be effective until this issue is resolved.

I think that one or both parties breaking one of these two commandments is the root of almost every marriage issue. Any connection has the same limitations. We are doomed to failure the moment we start prioritizing our needs and wishes above those of God or our spouse.

Are there issues with communicating in your marriage? How often do you listen to what your spouse (or God) has to say rather than arguing for more time? Feeling your partner's animosity and bitterness growing? When was the last time you prayed for him or her and thanked God for your connection? Having trouble getting some quality time together? What if you and your partner prayed and asked God for guidance on how to spend your time?

You'll find that when you start to perform these things, your attention naturally begins to turn away from yourself and your wants and toward God and your spouse.

As a consequence, communication issues start to get better, resentment and anger start to disappear, and you naturally want to spend more time together. Of course, you can't anticipate such changes to occur immediately. In addition, your partnership will inevitably run into troubles with finances, child raising, and other uncontrollable factors.

However, your marriage will be able to withstand any storm if you dedicate your union to God and consciously choose each day to put God and your spouse above everything else. Additionally, you'll have a great time traveling together.

www.ingramcontent.com/pod-product-compliance
Lightning Source LLC
LaVergne TN
LVHW020528160826
845677LV00015B/3958

* 9 7 9 8 3 5 3 5 0 1 3 2 9 *